Salmon

and Other Bony Fish

Editor in Chief: Paul A. Kobasa
Supplementary Publications: Christine Sullivan, Scott Thomas
Research: Cheryl Graham
Graphics and Design: Sandra Dyrlund, Charlene Epple
Permissions: Janet Peterson
Prepress and Manufacturing: Carma Fazio, Anne Fritzinger, Steven Hueppchen, Tina Ramirez
Writer: Meish Goldish
Concept and Product Development: Editorial Options, Inc.
Series Designer: Karen Donica

For information about other World Book publications, visit our Web site at
http://www.worldbook.com or call 1-800-WORLDBK (967-5325).

For information about sales to schools and libraries, call 1-800-975-3250 (United States);
1-800-837-5365 (Canada).

World Book, Inc.
233 N. Michigan Avenue
Chicago, IL 60601

The Library of Congress has catalogued an earlier edition of this title as follows:

Goldish, Meish.
    Salmon and other bony fish.
      p. cm. -- (World Book's animals of the world)
    Summary: Presents information about the physical characteristics, habits, and behavior
of salmon and such related fish as eels, flounder, swordfish, and piranhas.
    ISBN 0-7166-1229-1 -- ISBN 0-7166-1223-2 (set)
    1. Salmon--Juvenile literature. 2. Osteichthyes--Juvenile literature. [1. Salmon. 2.
Fishes.] I. Title. II. Series.

    QL638.S2 G65 2002
    597--dc21
                                        2001046713

This edition:
Set 3 ISBN-13: 978-0-7166-1352-7   Set 3 ISBN-10: 0-7166-1352-2
Salmon ISBN-13: 978-0-7166-1358-9   Salmon ISBN-10: 0-7166-1358-1

Printed in Malaysia
3 4 5 6 7 8 9 09 08 07 06

Picture Acknowledgments: Cover: © Herve Berthoule, Jacana, Photo Researchers; © Jane Burton, Bruce Coleman Inc.; © Tom McHugh, Photo Researchers; © Hans Reinhard, Bruce Coleman Collection.

© James Allen, Bruce Coleman Inc. 25; © Charles V. Angelo, Photo Researchers 57; © Herve Berthoule, Jacana, Photo Researchers 3, 13; © Werner Bertsch, Bruce Coleman Inc. 9; © Jane Burton, Bruce Coleman Inc. 5, 41, 45; © Tui DeRoy, Bruce Coleman Inc. 9; © Jeff Foott, Bruce Coleman Inc. 17, 19; © Francois Gohier, Photo Researchers 23; © Bud Lehnhausen, Photo Researchers 7; © Zig Leszczynski, Animals Animals 35; © Larry Lipsky, Bruce Coleman Inc. 39, 43; © Andrew J. Martinez, Photo Researchers 33; © Tom McHugh, Photo Researchers 51; © Chris McLaughlin, Animals Animals 5, 49; © Gary Milburn, Tom Stack & Associates 21; © Brian Miller, Bruce Coleman Inc. 9; © Charles E. Mohr, Photo Researchers 59; © Mark Newman, Photo Researchers 15; © Hans Reinhard, Bruce Coleman Inc. 9, 29; © Hans Reinhard, Bruce Coleman Collection 31; © Alvin E. Steffan, Photo Researchers 55; © Kim Taylor, Bruce Coleman Collection 37, 53; © Kim Taylor, Bruce Coleman Inc. 27; © Ronald Thomason, Bruce Coleman Inc. 61; © Norbert Wu 47.

Illustrations: WORLD BOOK illustration by Michael DiGiorgio 11, WORLD BOOK illustration by Kersti Mack 62.

World Book's Animals of the World

Salmon
and Other Bony Fish

World Book, Inc.
A Scott Fetzer company
Chicago

Contents

What Is a Bony Fish?

Fish are vertebrates *(VUR tuh brihts)*, which are animals with backbones. Fish live in water and usually breathe with gills. A bony fish is a fish whose skeleton is made mostly of bone. Salmon and trout are bony fish. Bass, catfish, flounder, barracuda *(BAIR uh KOO duh)*, and seahorses are bony fish, too.

Altogether, there are about 24,600 kinds of fish. Most of these fish have bones. In fact, there are about 23,700 kinds of bony fish. But some fish, including sharks and their relatives, have no bones at all. Instead they have skeletons made of a tough, rubbery material called cartilage *(KAHR tuh lihj)*.

Salmon

Where in the World Do Bony Fish Live?

Bony fish live almost anywhere there is water. They are found in chilly waters in the Arctic and in warm waters in the tropics. Bony fish swim in streams, rivers, lakes, and oceans. Salmon are bony fish that usually grow up in streams, but they spend their adult lives in the ocean.

Most adult salmon live along the coast of the North Pacific Ocean. These include the chinook *(chuh NOOK),* chum, coho, pink, and sockeye salmon. Amago and cherry salmon are found in the Pacific waters of eastern Asia. Only one kind of salmon, the Atlantic salmon, swims in the Atlantic Ocean.

A few groups of salmon live their entire lives in northern lakes and streams that don't flow to the ocean. People have released freshwater salmon into other lakes around the world. There they have become popular sport fish.

Arctic waters

Tropical waters

Stream

Lake

What Makes a Salmon a Bony Fish?

A salmon is a bony fish because its skeleton is made mostly of bone. The skull, backbone, and ribs are made of bone. Salmon and most other bony fish also have many thin bones, called rays, inside their fins.

Skull bones form the frame for a salmon's head. The skull bones include the upper and lower jaw and the brain case. Bony plates protect the gills that are located on the side of a salmon's head.

The backbone forms the frame for the rest of a salmon's body. The backbone has many separate pieces of bone called *vertebrae (VUR tuh bree).* The ribs are attached to the vertebrae.

Bony fin rays form the frame for a salmon's fins. Fins help the fish swim and keep its balance.

Diagram of a Salmon

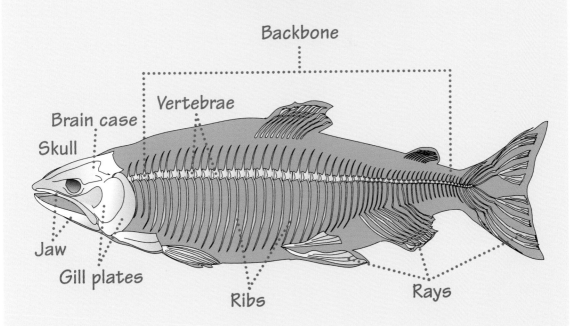

Backbone

Vertebrae

Brain case

Skull

Jaw

Gill plates

Ribs

Rays

11

What Do Adult Salmon Look Like?

Adult salmon are shaped a bit like torpedoes so that they can easily dart through the water. An adult salmon has six kinds of fins. The smallest fin is called the *adipose (AD uh pohs) fin*. It's located on top of the body, near the caudal *(KAW duhl)* fin.

Hard, shiny scales cover the salmon's skin and protect its body. Most adult salmon found in the ocean have dark-colored backs and silvery-white bellies.

Typical salmon grow to a length of about 2 feet (61 centimeters) and weigh about 10 pounds (4.5 kilograms). But chinook salmon can grow much bigger. Chinook salmon can reach 3 feet (91 centimeters) long and weigh over 100 pounds (45 kilograms). That's why chinook salmon are also known as king salmon.

A Salmon's Fins

Dorsal fin

Adipose fin

Caudal fin

Pectoral fins

Pelvic fins

Anal fin

Where Are Baby Salmon Born?

Most adult salmon live in the salty ocean. In the summer and fall, however, they swim up a freshwater stream to spawn, or mate. That's where the females lay their eggs.

Soon after the adult salmon arrive, the female digs a redd, or nest. She does this by slapping her tail hard on the gravel bottom. When the redd is finished, the female lays her round, pink eggs. As the eggs are laid, a male fertilizes them.

After the redd is filled with fertilized eggs, the female swims a little farther and digs a new redd. As she digs, she stirs up gravel with her tail. The current carries the gravel over the old redd. There the gravel settles and protects the eggs. Altogether, a female salmon may lay between 2,000 and 17,000 eggs, depending on her size. That's a lot of eggs!

Spawning salmon

How Do Baby Salmon Grow?

Baby salmon first grow inside eggs. They use the yellow-orange yolks in the eggs as food. After two to four months, the babies hatch out of the eggs.

After hatching, the baby salmon are called *alevins (AL uh vihnz).* They stay in their nests for several weeks or months. During this time, these tiny salmon still have yolk sacs attached to their bodies that supply them with food.

While in the nest, an alevin smells the water around it. Specific rocks, plants, and chemicals in the stream give the water its smell. And no other stream has the exact same smell. An alevin remembers this smell and never forgets it. When it is an adult, a salmon uses the smell to return to the exact same stream to spawn.

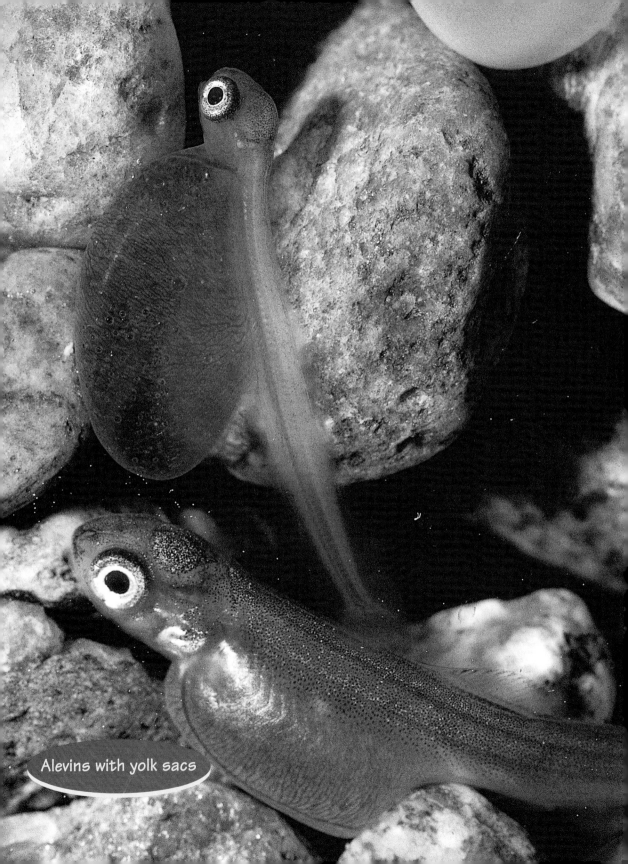

Alevins with yolk sacs

What Is a Salmon Fry?

A salmon fry sounds like a fish dinner, but it's actually the name for a young salmon. By the spring, a baby salmon is big enough to leave its nest. When it is ready to do this, it is called a fry. A fry is about 1 inch (2.5 centimeters) long.

The yolk sac that had fed the alevin until this point is gone. Now the fry must start to look for food. It eats insects and small water organisms called plankton. Fry must be careful because trout and other big fish eat them. Hungry ducks, herons, kingfishers, and sea gulls do, too. The fry starts to grow scales on its skin to protect its body. Most salmon fry also develop spots called *parr marks*. These spots help fry hide in the rocky stream. Even so, many of them are caught and eaten.

The fry of some kinds of salmon stay in fresh water for only a few days. Then they start their long swim to the salty ocean. The fry of other kinds of salmon stay in fresh water much longer before heading to the ocean.

18

Salmon fry

When Is a Salmon a Smolt?

A salmon becomes a smolt when it swims from its freshwater stream and heads to the ocean.

A smolt's body goes through many changes as it makes this journey. It loses its parr marks. It turns dark on top and silvery-white on its sides and belly. Its new colors help the smolt hide in the ocean. From above, a smolt's dark top will be hard to see against the deep blue waters of the ocean. And from below, a smolt's silvery-white belly will be hard to see against light shining down through the water.

Changes also take place inside the young salmon. Its kidneys and gills become very good at getting rid of large amounts of salt. This will come in handy in the smolt's new ocean home. Many smolt actually wait at or near the mouths of streams or rivers for several months. This water is less salty than water farther out in the ocean. Waiting here gives a smolt's body time to get used to the change.

Salmon smolt

How Do Salmon Return Home?

When adult salmon are ready to spawn, they return to their home streams. Salmon use their sense of smell to help guide them back to the same stream where they hatched.

On their journey home, adult salmon make many changes—much as they did on their first trip to the ocean. Most salmon change color to attract a mate. Adult chinook salmon turn from silvery-white to brownish-red. Sockeye salmon turn from silver to bright red. Most salmon also stop eating and focus on their journey.

The trip home is very hard. It can take several weeks, and it can cover 2,000 miles (3,200 kilometers). The salmon must swim upstream, against the water current. They leap high over big rocks and waterfalls. Some become weak or get injured and die along the way. For most kinds of salmon, even those that survive the trip die after they spawn.

Sockeye salmon leaping

What Dangers Do Salmon Face?

Salmon face many dangers. Birds and fish eat salmon eggs, fry, and smolt. Some salmon never get to the ocean because they die along the way. Water pollution is also dangerous for salmon, especially smolt.

A salmon that reaches the sea may be too big for herons or other small birds, but it had better watch out for eagles or ospreys. An adult salmon's other enemies include bears, sea lions, seals, and killer whales. Many salmon are also caught in large fishing nets.

Salmon that survive in the ocean grow bigger. They eat many sea animals, including shrimp, squid, and other fish. Some kinds of salmon may stay and grow in the ocean for only six months before they return home to spawn. Other kinds may live in the sea for six years or more.

Bear preying on salmon

Which Fish Are the Closest Relatives of Salmon?

The closest relatives of salmon are trout. Trout and salmon belong to the same family, or group, of bony fish. They have similar, torpedolike shapes. Both fish have small adipose fins. Some trout and salmon look so much alike that they are often mistaken for each other.

The best-known trout is the rainbow trout. It is closely related to salmon that live in the Pacific Ocean. Like salmon, rainbow trout spawn in streams. Some rainbow trout also travel to the ocean. A rainbow trout that makes this journey is called a steelhead. Most rainbow trout, however, stay in freshwater streams all their lives.

Rainbow trout are named for their colorful reddish bands that run along their sides. These trout also have black spots on their upper bodies and tails. Rainbow trout that stay in streams usually weigh around 2 to 5 pounds (1 to 2.3 kilograms).

Rainbow trout

What Fish Can Breathe Out of Water?

Actually, many fish can breathe out of water. But none is better at it than a lungfish is. A lungfish breathes out of water by using a lunglike organ called a swim bladder. Some kinds of lungfish can even survive in dried-up rivers for weeks or months.

Most lungfish, like the South American lungfish you see here, have gills that are poorly developed. They breathe air mostly with their swim bladders. If one of these lungfish couldn't reach the water's surface, it would drown. However, the Australian lungfish breathes mostly with its gills. It gulps air at the water's surface only when the water doesn't have much oxygen in it.

Lungfish are one of a few bony fish that are able to control their fins as land animals control their limbs. Most fish can only raise or lower their fin rays. But a lungfish has joints that attach the fins to its body just as arms and legs are attached to a person's body.

South American
lungfish

Are Catfish Related to Cats?

No, but a catfish has whiskers that look like those of a cat! The whiskers are called *barbels*. Catfish, like these bluespotted corydoras *(kuh RIH duh ruhs)*, use their barbels to find food and feel their way around.

Most catfish live in freshwater lakes, ponds, and streams. Some kinds of catfish live in the ocean. Catfish usually eat insects, frogs, and other water animals. Larger catfish eat other fish.

Catfish vary in size. The largest is the European catfish or wels. It may grow to more than 10 feet (3 meters) long and weigh 400 pounds (180 kilograms). It belongs to the same family as the glass catfish. This bony fish is only 4 inches (10 centimeters) long.

The most unusual catfish is the walking catfish, found in Asia. It can crawl on land from one lake or pond to another by raising itself up with its front fins and pushing with its tail. It's a good thing that a walking catfish can breathe out of water as a lungfish does!

Bluespotted corydoras

Are Eels Snakes or Fish?

Eels may look like snakes, but they aren't related to those slithery reptiles at all. Eels are actually fish. There are about 700 kinds of eels, and most spend all their lives in the ocean.

Eels that are in the family known as common or freshwater eels spend part of their lives in fresh water. Common eels include the American eel and the European eel. Most male common eels grow to about 1 1/2 feet (46 centimeters) long. Most females grow 3 to 4 feet (91 to 122 centimeters) long.

American and European eels lay their eggs in the Sargasso *(sahr GAS oh)* Sea, a part of the Atlantic Ocean. As the young eels hatch and grow, ocean currents carry them northward to the coast of North America or Europe. These eels spend most of their adult life in the lakes, rivers, and streams of these two continents. When they are ready to spawn, the eels return to the sea.

American eel

How Shocking Is an Electric Eel?

You might be shocked to find out that, despite its name and looks, an electric eel is not an eel at all! It belongs to a family of bony fish known as knifefish. Even though it's not an eel, an electric eel's name isn't all wrong. An electric eel does produce strong electric charges. Each charge is about 500 volts. That's enough power to stun a person or to kill a small fish.

An electric eel has three pairs of electric organs on each side of its body. Each organ has thousands of muscle cells. The cells give off small bursts of electricity after a nerve sets them off. Each burst lasts about 1/500 of a second. It is short but powerful!

Electric eels live in muddy rivers in South America. They grow to 8 feet (2.4 meters) long.

Electric eel

Can a Flyingfish Really Fly?

No, but a flyingfish can glide a long way. A flyingfish uses its strong tail to push itself up out of water. In the air, the fish spreads its large fins so they act as wings. However, a flyingfish doesn't flap its fins as a bird flaps its wings. Instead, a flyingfish uses its fins to glide through the air. It can glide as far as 1,000 feet (300 meters). That may be enough to escape a predator swimming in the water below.

There are more than 50 kinds of flyingfish. Fourwing flyingfish are so named because they have long pectoral and pelvic fins. These fins are so big that they look like four "wings."

If you go sailing on the Atlantic or Pacific ocean, watch out for flyingfish. Sometimes they fly right into boats!

Fourwing flyingfish

Why Does a Flounder Change Colors?

A flounder changes color to hide from enemies and to surprise its prey. A flounder lives at the bottom of the sea. Lying flat on its side, a flounder can change its color and pattern to match the sea floor. For example, if a flounder is lying on a sandy area, its markings begin to look like grains of sand.

After a flounder settles on the ocean floor, it wiggles its fins. The motion stirs up sand and shells. The sand and shells settle on the edges of the flounder's body. That makes the flounder even harder to see.

When it hatches, a flounder looks about the same as a small salmon. As it grows, its body becomes thin and flat. One eye moves to the other side of the head. This helps a flounder see better when lying on the ocean floor.

38

Gulf flounder

Why Does a Porcupinefish Puff Up?

A porcupinefish inflates, or puffs up, to protect itself. The fish has flat, needlelike spines all over its body. If an enemy scares it, the porcupinefish swallows water and blows up like a balloon.

When a porcupinefish is scared, it puffs up to two or three times its normal size. It doesn't get any longer, but it sure gets big around! Not only can its large size scare away an enemy, but its spines now stick straight out. Most enemies don't dare touch the porcupinefish then! Once danger has passed, the fish shrinks to its normal size.

Porcupinefish are about 10 to 12 inches (25 to 30 centimeters) long and live in the warm waters of the Atlantic, Pacific, and Indian oceans. These fish eat snails, crabs, and sea urchins.

Porcupinefish,
inflated and deflated

Which Bony Fish Sound Like Drums?

Fish called drums are named for the sounds they make. When drums tighten their stomach muscles, the muscles vibrate against their swim bladders. These vibrations cause loud drumming sounds. A fish's swim bladder helps it float in water rather than sink to the bottom.

There are about 250 kinds of drums. Many live in shallow ocean waters near the shore. The spotted drum is a common drum that spends its life in tropical waters in the Caribbean.

Drums vary in size. The spotted drum usually grows about 9 inches (23 centimeters) long. The biggest drum is the totoaba *(toh TWAH vuh),* in the Gulf of California. It grows up to 6 feet (1.8 meters) and weighs up to 225 pounds (101 kilograms).

Spotted drum

Which Bony Fish Looks as if It Has a Horse's Head?

A seahorse, of course! This fish gets its name because its head looks like that of a tiny horse. From head to tail, an average seahorse is less than 6 inches (15 centimeters) long. A seahorse is a bony fish that lives in shallow, warm seas.

A seahorse's body is made of bony plates. The fish's tail is long and can bend. A seahorse uses its tail to grab onto plants. That way the tiny fish can stay in one place in the water and not get swept away by the current. Sometimes, a group of baby seahorses grab each other's tails to stay together.

Seahorses give birth to their young in a very unusual way. The female lays hundreds of eggs in the male's pouch. The male carries the eggs for 10 to 45 days. Then the tiny babies swim out of papa!

Seahorse

How Does a Swordfish Use Its Sword?

A swordfish has a long, flat upper jaw that looks like a sword. Scientists believe it may use its sword to break up groups of fish. Then the swordfish can attack the fish one at a time. The swordfish may also use its sword as an aid in swimming. The sword breaks the flow of water, making it easier for the sword fish to swim.

Swordfish are found in warm ocean waters. They are one of the fastest kinds of fish. They can slice through water up to 60 miles (97 kilometers) an hour.

The sword on a swordfish is about one-third as long as its body. Most swordfish are 5 to 8 feet (1.5 to 2.4 meters) long. They weigh about 150 to 300 pounds (70 to 135 kilograms).

Swordfish

What Makes a Barracuda So Scary?

A barracuda is scary because it has large jaws and very sharp teeth. It eats lots of other fish in the sea. If a barracuda feels threatened, it will even attack a person.

The biggest and most feared barracuda is the great barracuda. It is called "the tiger of the sea" because it is so big and dangerous. The great barracuda grows to 6 feet (1.8 meters) and weighs up to 100 pounds (45 kilograms). It swims in the Atlantic, Indian, and Pacific oceans.

Great barracuda

Are Piranhas Really Dangerous?

Piranhas *(pih RAHN yuhz)* have triangle-shaped teeth that are razor-sharp. The fish are known as cruel killers. Sometimes they swim in large schools. They may attack a large fish or other animal in the water. The piranhas will use their sharp teeth to chop their victim into tiny bits.

However, piranhas are not always that deadly. In fact, they usually swim alone. They eat small fish as well as seeds and fruits that fall into the water. Piranhas rarely attack people.

Piranhas swim in rivers and lakes in South America. And they are kept as pets around the world. Because they eat so much and can be expensive to feed, some pet owners have released them into local waters. This practice has introduced piranhas to habitats outside their native range. In these new environments, many piranhas have eaten large numbers of fish, frogs, and other water animals.

School of piranhas

Why Does an Archerfish Shoot Water?

An archerfish shoots drops of water to catch its prey. The fish has an excellent aim. It shoots at insects on plants that hang over the water. It also shoots at spiders that have spun their webs above the water. When a victim is hit by the drops, it falls into the water and the archerfish gets a meal!

An archerfish shoots water by squeezing its gill covers. That pushes water forward along the roof of its mouth. The stream of water can fly more than 3 feet (90 centimeters) in the air.

Archerfish live in fresh or slightly salty water in southeastern Asia and in Australia. Most archerfish are about 6 inches (15 centimeters) long. Some grow as long as 16 inches (41 centimeters).

Archerfish shooting
water at victim

Why Are Sunfish Named After the Sun?

Sunfish are named after the sun because many of them are round and brightly colored—just like the sun! Sunfish such as the bluegill and pumpkinseed have bright yellow or orange bellies. Sunfish make up a family of about 30 freshwater fish.

These bony fish live in lakes and streams across North America. Most sunfish grow to only 8 inches (20 centimeters) long and weigh under 1 pound (454 grams). Other members of this family, including largemouth bass, can grow up to 2 feet (61 centimeters) long and weigh over 15 pounds (6.8 kilograms).

Beware of the name *sunfish*, however. It also refers to a group of strange-looking ocean fish with giant heads. They are also known as molas. These fish often rest on the surface of the water in sunny weather. Unlike freshwater sunfish, these ocean sunfish weigh 1,000 pounds (450 kilograms)!

Bluegill

Which Fish Have Their Own Fishing Rods?

Anglerfish do! Each anglerfish, like this longlure frogfish, has a long "rod" that is actually a fin ray. The fin ray looks like a worm. An anglerfish uses the fin ray to "fish" for other fish.

An anglerfish sits on the sea floor, looking like its surroundings. The only part of its body that other fish often notice is the fin ray. The anglerfish dangles the ray in front of its mouth. When another fish sees the ray, it swims closer and the anglerfish gobbles it up!

Some kinds of anglerfish can fish for other fish even in the dark. That's because their fin rays make their own light. The light attracts victims, and the anglerfish get a snack in the dark.

Longlure frogfish

Which Bony Fish Can't See?

A cavefish, or blindfish, has no eyes. It also has no skin color. A cavefish looks pink because its blood shows through its flesh.

Cavefish spend their entire lives in pools of water in caves in the eastern United States. Cavefish are only about 5 inches (13 centimeters) long. They may not be able to see, but they do have excellent senses of touch. Their bodies have rows of skin growths that they use to feel their way around and to find food.

Besides cavefish, there are about 20 other kinds of fish that can't see. These fish live in caves and deep seas around the world.

Cavefish

Are Bony Fish in Danger?

All bony fish, except the largest ones, are always in danger of being eaten by other fish and water animals. Many fish are also in danger of being caught by people.

Salmon is a popular food for people. Each year, fishers from Canada, Norway, Japan, the United States, Chile, and Russia catch millions of salmon. As a result, some types of salmon are now endangered.

To protect the fish, laws now limit salmon fishing in some parts of the world. This allows many salmon to survive in order to spawn. Also, thousands of salmon are now raised in hatcheries and then released into rivers and streams.

Salmon

Bony Fish Fun Facts

→ The name *salmon* means "leaper" in Latin. Salmon leap as high as 10 feet (3 meters) over waterfalls when swimming upstream.

→ If a porcupinefish is held out of the water, it can puff itself up by swallowing air.

→ In Canada and Alaska, sockeye salmon that spend their entire lives in freshwater lakes and streams are known as kokanee.

→ The longest swordfish ever caught was nearly 15 feet (4.6 meters) long and weighed 1,430 pounds (650 kilograms).

→ The world's smallest bony fish is the *Trimmatom nanus* of the Indian Ocean. It is only 2/5 inch (1 centimeter) long.

→ There are more kinds of fish than all other kinds of vertebrates on water and land combined.

Glossary

adipose fin A small fin located near the tail and on the top of some kinds of fish.

alevin A newly hatched salmon.

barbel A whisker on a catfish.

cartilage A tough, rubbery material that forms the skeleton of some kinds of fish.

caudal fin A fin located at the back end of a fish; the "tail fin."

fertilize To unite with an egg cell.

fin A movable fanlike part of a fish.

fry A young salmon after it leaves its nest.

gills Organs that many kinds of fish use to breathe.

hatchery A place created by humans for fish eggs to hatch.

parr marks Coloration on a salmon fry that help the fish blend in with its surroundings.

plankton Very small organisms that float in seas and lakes.

rays Thin bones inside the fins of some kinds of fish.

school A large group of fish.

smolt A young salmon as it swims from a stream to the ocean.

spawn To mate; to lay eggs.

swim bladder An organ that helps keep fish afloat.

vertebrae Tiny bones that make up a bony fish's backbone.

vertebrate An animal with a backbone.

volt The unit for measuring the force of electricity.

yolk The internal part of an egg that serves as food for the young before it hatches.

yolk sac A baglike structure containing food materials.

Index

(**Boldface** indicates a photo or illustration.)

For more information about Salmon and Other Bony Fish, try these resources:

Classifying Fish, by Richard and Louise Spilsbury,
    Heinemann Library, 2003
Incredible Fish, by John Townsend, Raintree, 2005
Life of a Salmon, by Clare Hibbert, Raintree, 2005

http://salmonpage.com
http://www.adfg.state.ak.us/pubs/notebook/fish/
coho.php
http://www.enchantedlearning.com/subjects/fish/
printouts/bonyfish.shtml

Bony Fishes Classification

Scientists classify animals by placing them into groups. The animal kingdom is a group that contains all the world's animals. Phylum, class, order, and family are smaller groups. Each phylum contains many classes. A class contains orders, an order contains families, and a family contains individual species. Each species also has its own scientific name. Here is how the animals in this book fit in to this system.

Animals with backbones and their relatives (Phylum Chordata)

Bony fishes (Classes Sarcopterygii and Actinopterygii)

Anglerfishes (Order Lophiiformes)

Frogfishes (Family Antennariidae)
Longlure frogfish . . . . *Antennarius multiocellatus*

Australian lungfish (Order Ceratodontiformes)

Australian lungfish (Family Ceratodontidae)
Australian lungfish . . . . *Neoceratodus forsteri*

Catfishes (Order Siluriformes)

Bluespotted corydoras and its relatives (Family Callichthyidae)
Bluespotted corydoras . . . . *Corydoras melanistius*

European (wels) catfish and its relatives (Family Siluridae)
European (wels) catfish . . . . *Silurus glanis*
Glass catfish . . . . *Kryptopterus bicirrhis*

Walking catfish and its relatives (Family Clariidae)
Walking catfish . . . . *Clarias batrachus*

Cavefishes and their relatives (Order Percopsiformes)

Cavefishes (Family Amblyopsidae)

Eels (Order Anguilliformes)

Common (freshwater) eels (Family Anguillidae)
American eel . . . . *Anguilla rostrata*
European eel . . . . *Anguilla anguilla*

Flounders and their relatives (Order Pleuronectiformes)

Gulf flounder and its relatives (Family Paralichthyidae)
Gulf flounder . . . . *Paralichthys albigutta*

Flyingfishes and their relatives (Order Beloniformes)

Flyingfishes (Family Exocoetidae)
Fourwing flyingfish . . . . *Hirundichthys affinis*

Knifefishes (Order Gymnotiformes)

Electric eel (Family Electrophoridae)
Electric eel. . . . . *Electrophorus electricus*

Perches and their relatives (Order Perciformes)

Archerfishes (Family Toxotidae)

Barracudas (Family Sphyraenidae)
Great barracuda . . . . *Sphyraena barracuda*

Drums (Family Sciaenidae)
Spotted drum . . . . *Equetus punctatus*
Totoaba . . . . *Totoaba macdonaldi*

Perches (Family Percidae)

Sunfishes (Family Centrarchidae)
Bluegill . . . . *Lepomis macrochirus*
Largemouth bass. . . . . *Micropterus salmoides*
Pumpkinseed. . . . . *Lepomis gibbosus*

Swordfishes (Family Xiphiidae)
Swordfish . . . . *Xiphias gladius*

Piranhas and their relatives (Order Characiformes)

Piranhas and their relatives (Family Characidae)

Porcupinefishes and their relatives (Order Tetraodontiformes)

Porcupinefishes (Family Diodontidae)

Ocean sunfishes (molas) (Family Molidae)

Salmon, trout, and their relatives (Order Salmoniformes)

Salmon, trout, and their relatives (Family Salmonidae)
Amago salmon . . . . *Oncorhynchus masou rhodurus*
Atlantic salmon . . . . *Salmo salar*
Chinook (king) salmon. . . . . . . *Oncorhynchus tshawytscha*
Cherry salmon. . . . . *Oncorhynchus masou masou*
Chum salmon . . . . *Oncorhynchus keta*
Coho salmon. . . . . *Oncorhynchus kisutch*
Pink salmon . . . . *Oncorhynchus gorbuscha*
Rainbow trout (steelhead. . . . . . *Oncorhynchus mykiss*
Sockeye (kokanee) salmon . . . . *Oncorhynchus nerka*

Seahorses and their relatives (Order Gasterosteiformes)

Seahorses and their relatives (Family Syngnathidae)

South American lungfish and its relatives (Order Lepidosireniformes)

South American lungfish (Family Lepidosirenidae)
South American lungfish . . . . . . *Lepidosiren paradoxa*

Usually, the plural of *fish* is *fish*. However, when referring to more than one species by name, the plural should be *fishes*. For simplicity, however, throughout this book we've used the simpler plural *fish* with the exception of this scientific classification chart.